Thrifting Your Way to a 6-figure reselling business

Table of Contents

Chapter 1: The Reseller's Mindset: Seeing Value Where Others Don't — 4

Chapter 2: Mastering the Art of the Thrift Store Hunt — 9

Chapter 3: Beyond Goodwill: Unconventional Sourcing Strategies — 17

Chapter 4: Pricing for Profit: Maximizing Your Margins — 26

Chapter 5: Building Your Brand: Standing Out in a Crowded Market — 36

Chapter 6: The Power of Niche: Finding Your Reselling Sweet Spot — 46

Chapter 7: Inventory Management: From Spare Room to Warehouse — 56

Chapter 8: Shipping and Handling: Streamlining Your Fulfillment Process — 66

Chapter 9: Customer Service: Turning Buyers into Repeat Customers — 77

Chapter 10: Scaling Up: From Side Hustle to Full-Time Business — 88

Chapter 11: Leveraging Social Media for Sales and Marketing 99

Chapter 12: Financial Management: Tracking Profits and
Planning for Growth   110

Chapter 13: Navigating Legal and Tax Considerations for
Resellers   121

Chapter 14: Advanced Flipping: Restoring and Upcycling for
Higher Profits   132

Chapter 15: Building a Team: When and How to Hire Help   142

Chapter 1: The Reseller's Mindset: Seeing Value Where Others Don't

Picture this: You're standing in a dimly lit thrift store, surrounded by mountains of cast-off junk. To the average person, it's a wasteland of unwanted items. But to you? It's a goldmine waiting to be unearthed.

That's the reseller's mindset.

It's not just about having a keen eye for brand names or spotting the occasional diamond in the rough. It's about rewiring your brain to see potential where others see trash. It's about understanding that value isn't just about what something cost originally, but what someone out there is willing to pay for it right now.

So how do you cultivate this mindset? It starts with curiosity.

Every item has a story. That dusty old camera? It could be a vintage treasure sought after by collectors. Those funky 80s earrings? They might be the missing piece in someone's retro costume. That ratty-looking book? It could be a rare first edition.

But here's the kicker: You don't need to be an expert in everything. You just need to know enough to ask the right questions. Is this old? Is it rare? Is it useful? Is it beautiful to someone?

Let's break it down:

1. **Embrace the unknown:** Half the fun (and profit) in this business comes from stumbling upon items you've never seen before. Don't shy

away from the weird and wonderful. Research is your friend.

2. Think like your buyer: You're not just selling items; you're selling solutions to problems, missing pieces to collections, or the thrill of owning something unique. Put yourself in your potential customers' shoes.

3. Quality over quantity: Sure, you could flip a bunch of $5 items for $10 each. But the real money? It's in finding that one $50 item you can sell for $500.

4. Patience pays off: The reseller's mindset isn't about get-rich-quick schemes. It's about playing the long game. Sometimes, holding onto an item for the right buyer can mean the difference between a decent profit and a spectacular one.

5. Learn from your mistakes: You will buy duds. You will overpay sometimes. Don't beat yourself up. Each misstep is a lesson that'll make you sharper for the next find.

Remember, developing this mindset takes time. It's like training a muscle. The more you exercise it, the stronger it gets. Soon, you'll find yourself automatically scanning rooms for hidden treasures, whether you're at a yard sale or a fancy dinner party (just try not to obviously price-check the host's decor on your phone).

In the chapters to come, we'll dig into the nitty-gritty of where to source, how to price, and how to sell. But none of that matters if you don't first master the art of seeing value where others don't.

So next time you're about to toss out that "junk" in your attic, pause. Look at it with fresh eyes. Ask yourself: "Could this be someone's treasure?" That pause, that question - that's the first step towards your six-figure reselling business.

Chapter 2: Mastering the Art of the Thrift Store Hunt

Alright, treasure hunters. You've got the mindset. Now it's time to put boots on the ground.

Welcome to the wild world of thrift store hunting.

First things first: Forget everything you think you know about shopping. This isn't a leisurely stroll through a mall. This is a mission. You're not a customer; you're an archaeologist of value, and every thrift store is your dig site.

Let's break down the anatomy of a successful thrift store hunt:

Timing is Everything

Early bird gets the worm? Sometimes. But the night owl might catch a gem too. Many thrift stores restock throughout the day. Some even wait until closing time to put out fresh inventory. Get friendly with the staff (more on that later) and learn their restocking schedule.

Pro tip: Hit the stores on weekdays. Weekends are amateur hour.

The Art of the Scan

Walk in. Take a deep breath. Now, scan.

Don't get bogged down in one section. Your first pass should be quick, like a predator surveying its hunting ground. Look for anything that catches your eye: unusual shapes, bright colors, brand names peeking out.

Got it? Good. Now do it again. And again. You'd be amazed how many gems you miss on the first pass.

Know Your Sections (But Don't Be Bound By Them)

Sure, men's shirts are in the men's section. Usually. But sometimes, a clueless donor or rushed employee might stick a vintage Levi's jacket in with the women's coats. Or toss a valuable first edition in the kids' book bin.

Cross-pollinate your searches. That "ugly" holiday sweater in XXL? It might be a sought-after vintage piece for the right buyer.

The Touch Test

Use your hands, not just your eyes. Quality often reveals itself through touch. That "boring" black sweater? It might be cashmere. That heavy jacket? Could be real leather.

Develop a feel for different materials. It'll save you time and help you spot high-value items faster.

Befriend the Staff

These folks are your secret weapon. They see everything that comes through those doors. A simple "Hey, seen anything cool lately?" can lead to insider info on fresh donations or upcoming sales.

But remember: They're not your personal shoppers. Be friendly, be grateful, and maybe bring them a coffee now and then. Kindness pays dividends in this business.

The Price Tag Isn't the Whole Story

That designer bag marked at $100? Might seem steep for a thrift store. But if it usually sells for $1000, you've struck gold.

Conversely, don't get starry-eyed over every $2 item. If you can't at least triple your money, it's probably not worth your time.

Always be calculating. Always be researching. Your phone is your best friend here.

The Unsexy Stuff

Everyone's hunting for designer clothes and vintage electronics. But you know what's really profitable? The boring stuff.

Printer ink. Craft supplies. Replacement parts for appliances. These might not be glamorous, but they sell. Fast.

Don't ignore the "junk" bins. One person's trash really is another person's treasure.

Trust Your Gut (But Verify)

Developed a hunch about an item? Follow it. But always, always double-check. That "designer" bag might be a knockoff. That "antique" might be a reproduction.

Use your phone to verify brands, check completed listings on eBay, and reverse image search anything suspicious.

The Exit Strategy

You've loaded up your cart. Now what?

Find a quiet corner and go through everything again. Be ruthless. Ask yourself: "Can I definitely make money on this?" If the answer isn't a resounding yes, put it back.

Remember, you're running a business, not building a personal collection.

The Golden Rule

Never leave empty-handed.

Seriously. Even if it's just one item, make it a rule to always find something with profit potential. This trains your eye and keeps you sharp.

Thrift store hunting is equal parts science and art. It's about developing systems, sure. But it's also about honing your instincts. The more you do it, the better you'll get.

So get out there. Happy hunting, reseller. Your next big score is waiting.

Chapter 3: Beyond Goodwill: Unconventional Sourcing Strategies

Listen up, reselling mavericks. We've covered the thrift store basics. Now it's time to kick it up a notch. Because let's face it - if you're only hitting up Goodwill, you're leaving money on the table.

It's time to get creative. To think outside the big-box thrift store. To go where other resellers fear to tread.

Ready? Let's dive into the wild world of unconventional sourcing.

Estate Sales: Where the Real Treasures Hide

First stop: estate sales. These are gold mines, folks. Why? Because you're often dealing with a lifetime's worth of accumulation. And here's the kicker - many estate sale organizers don't know what they've got.

Tips for conquering estate sales:

1. Get there early. Like, crack-of-dawn early. The good stuff goes fast.
2. Bring cash. And plenty of it.
3. Look for the overlooked. Everyone's fighting over the jewelry? Check out the garage or attic.
4. Be respectful. Remember, this was someone's home.

Pro tip: Make friends with estate sale companies. They might give you a heads up on upcoming sales.

Auctions: High Risk, High Reward

Auctions aren't for the faint of heart. But if you've got nerves of steel and a good eye, they can be incredibly lucrative.

Types to check out:
- Police auctions
- Storage unit auctions
- Farm auctions
- Government surplus auctions

The key? Do your homework. Know what things are worth before you start bidding. And set a hard limit. It's easy to get caught up in the excitement and overbid.

Flea Markets: Early Bird Special

Flea markets are like thrift stores on steroids. Here's how to crush it:

1. Arrive at the crack of dawn. Seriously.
2. Bring a flashlight. You might be shopping in the dark.
3. Look for vendors who are clearly not professional resellers.
4. Bundle deals are your friend. "How much for everything on this table?"

Remember: Haggling isn't just allowed, it's expected. Don't be shy.

Yard Sales: The Neighborhood Gold Rush

Yard sales can be hit or miss. But when they hit, oh boy.

Strategy time:
1. Map out a route the night before. Hit wealthy neighborhoods first.
2. Look for multi-family or community sales. More bang for your buck.

3. Go at the end of the day. Sellers are often willing to cut deals just to get rid of stuff.

Sneaky trick: Carry big bills. When you pull out a $100 for a $15 item, sellers often cut you a deal just to avoid making change.

Online Arbitrage: The Digital Frontier

Who says you need to leave your house to source inventory?

Places to look:
- Facebook Marketplace
- Craigslist
- eBay (yes, really)
- Local buy/sell groups

The secret sauce? Speed and persistence. Set up alerts. Be the first to respond. And always,

always check sold listings to know your potential profit margin.

Wholesale Liquidation: Go Big or Go Home

Ready to level up? Liquidation lots can be a game-changer.

But beware: This isn't for newbies. You need capital, storage space, and a solid understanding of your market.

Start small. Maybe a single pallet. Learn the ropes before you go all in on a truckload.

Dumpster Diving: One Person's Trash...

Okay, this isn't for everyone. But hear me out.

Some high-end stores throw out returns or slightly damaged items. Universities toss out good stuff during move-out week. And don't get me started on the treasures you can find behind electronics stores.

Just... check local laws first. And maybe bring hand sanitizer.

Build Your Network: The Human Touch

Here's a strategy most resellers overlook: Word of mouth.

Tell everyone what you do. Your hairdresser, your kid's teacher, that guy at the gym. You never know who's sitting on a goldmine in their attic.

Offer finder's fees. Create business cards. Become the person people think of when they want to offload stuff.

The Wildcard: Create Your Own Source

Why wait for inventory when you can create it?

Partner with local artists to sell their work. Find a manufacturer for that product idea you've been sitting on. Buy raw materials and upcycle them into something amazing.

The sky's the limit here, folks.

The Golden Rule of Sourcing

Never stop looking. Ever.

That random Tuesday afternoon when you're grabbing coffee? Swing by that new thrift store. Waiting for your kid's soccer practice to end? Scroll through Facebook Marketplace.

Opportunity doesn't punch a time clock. Neither should you.

Remember, the best resellers aren't just good at selling. They're sourcing ninjas. They see opportunities where others see junk. They zig when others zag.

Chapter 4: Pricing for Profit: Maximizing Your Margins

Alright, future tycoons of the reselling world. You've got the mindset. You've mastered the hunt. You've expanded your sourcing horizons. Now comes the million-dollar question (hopefully literally): How do you price your treasures?

Pricing. It's where fortunes are made—and lost. It's equal parts art and science, with a dash of psychology thrown in for good measure. Get it right, and you're rolling in dough. Get it wrong, and you're stuck with a garage full of unsold junk.

So buckle up, buttercup. We're about to turn you into a pricing pro.

The Golden Rule: Know Your Costs

Seems obvious, right? You'd be surprised how many newbies forget this. Your cost isn't just what you paid for the item. It's:

- Purchase price
- Gas for sourcing trips
- Shipping supplies
- Listing fees
- Payment processing fees
- Your time (yes, this counts!)

Add it all up. Now, here's the kicker: Your selling price needs to cover all of this, plus your desired profit margin. Speaking of which...

Profit Margins: Go Big or Go Home

In the reselling game, small margins are a recipe for failure. Why? Because you'll always have some items that don't sell, or sell for less than expected. You need the winners to cover the losers.

Aim for at least a 3x return on your investment. That vintage t-shirt you snagged for $5? It better sell for $15 or more. Otherwise, it's not worth your time.

But don't stop there. Look for those unicorns—the 10x, 20x, even 100x returns. They're out there. And they're what separates the six-figure resellers from the hobbyists.

Market Research: Your Secret Weapon

Before you price anything, do your homework. Check:

- eBay sold listings
- Poshmark sold items
- Amazon sales rank and pricing
- Specialty forums for niche items

Pro tip: Don't just look at current listings. Anyone can ask for the moon. Look at what actually sold. That's your real market value.

The Psychology of Pricing

Here's where it gets fun. Pricing isn't just about numbers. It's about perception.

- The power of 9: $39.99 feels cheaper than $40, even though it's basically the same.
- Anchor high: Start with a higher price. You can always lower it, but you can't raise it without looking sketchy.

- The rule of 100: For items under $100, use $.99 endings. Over $100? Use whole dollar amounts. It looks more "premium."

Remember: You're not just selling an item. You're selling a story, a feeling, a solution to a problem. Price accordingly.

Dynamic Pricing: Be Flexible, Get Rich

Static prices are for amateurs. Real reselling pros know that prices should fluctuate based on:

- Season (Christmas sweaters in July? Discount city. In November? Premium pricing, baby.)
- Supply and demand (Did that vintage band just announce a reunion tour? Jack up those t-shirt prices!)
- Platform (eBay buyers expect deals. Etsy buyers will pay premium for "unique" items.)

Don't be afraid to adjust prices. Regularly. It's not about finding the "right" price. It's about finding the right price right now.

Bundling: The Art of Selling More

Why sell one item when you can sell three? Bundling is a powerful tool in your pricing arsenal.

- Complementary items: Sold a vintage camera? Offer a bundle with film and a case.
- Bulk discounts: "Buy 2, get 1 50% off" can turn one sale into three.
- Mystery boxes: Great for clearing out slower-moving inventory.

Bundling isn't just about moving more product. It's about increasing your average order value. And that's where the real money is made.

The Low-Ball Offer: Friend or Foe?

You'll get them. A lot. Here's how to handle them:

1. Don't take it personally. It's business, not an insult to your mother.
2. Counter-offer. Always. Even if it's close to your asking price.
3. Use it as an opportunity to highlight value. "I can't go that low, but here's why it's worth my asking price..."

Sometimes, a low-ball offer can turn into a good sale. Other times, it's best to hold firm. Trust your gut.

When to Break the Rules

Here's the dirty secret of pricing: Sometimes, the "wrong" price is the right price.

- Loss leaders: Sell something cheap to get customers in the door.
- Building reputation: Sometimes, a smaller profit now leads to bigger profits later.
- Clearing inventory: If it's taking up space, sometimes any price is the right price.

The key? Know why you're breaking the rules. Make it a strategy, not a mistake.

The Ultimate Pricing Hack: Perceived Value

Want to know the real secret to pricing for massive profits? It's all about perceived value.

Don't just list an item. Sell an experience. That ratty old chair? It's not just furniture. It's a

"Mid-Century Modern Statement Piece Perfect for Your Instagram-Worthy Living Room."

Learn to write killer descriptions. Take amazing photos. Package your items like they're going to the Queen of England herself.

Because here's the truth: People don't buy things. They buy better versions of themselves.

The Bottom Line

Pricing isn't a set-it-and-forget-it thing. It's a skill. A muscle. The more you work it, the stronger it gets.

So experiment. Take risks. Learn from your mistakes (and your successes).

And always, always be willing to adjust. Because in the wild world of reselling, the only constant is change.

Chapter 5: Building Your Brand: Standing Out in a Crowded Market

Listen up, reselling rockstars. You've got the goods. You've priced them right. But in this dog-eat-dog world of online selling, that's not enough. You need to stand out. You need to be memorable. You need a brand.

"But wait," I hear you cry, "I'm just selling stuff online! Why do I need a brand?"

Oh, sweet summer child. Everyone has a brand. The question is: are you controlling yours, or is it controlling you?

Let's turn you from a faceless seller into a reselling sensation.

What's in a Name? Everything.

Your shop name is your handshake, your first impression, your chance to plant your flag in the reselling world. Choose wisely.

Some tips:
- Make it memorable
- Keep it relevant to what you're selling
- Ensure it's available across all platforms (consistency is key!)
- Avoid trendy spellings (looking at you, "Kool Findz")

Remember: You're not just picking a name. You're choosing your future empire's title. No pressure.

Logo Logic: More Than Just a Pretty Picture

You don't need to be Picasso to create a good logo. But you do need to think strategically.

Consider:
- Colors that reflect your brand's personality
- Simplicity (it should look good on a business card and a billboard)
- Versatility (will it work on light and dark backgrounds?)

Pro tip: If design isn't your forte, sites like Canva or even Fiverr can be your best friend. Don't be afraid to invest a little here. A good logo pays for itself.

Your Story: The Secret Sauce of Branding

Here's where the magic happens. Your story is what turns a casual browser into a loyal customer.

Are you a stay-at-home parent turning a hobby into a business? A vintage enthusiast sharing your passion with the world? A sustainability warrior giving pre-loved items new homes?

Whatever it is, own it. Share it. Make it part of every interaction.

But remember: Authenticity is key. Don't fabricate a story. Customers can smell BS from a mile away.

Photography: A Picture's Worth a Thousand Sales

In the world of online reselling, your photos are your storefront. They're not just showing the item; they're selling a lifestyle.

Some non-negotiables:
- Clean, uncluttered backgrounds

- Multiple angles
- Close-ups of any flaws or special features
- Lifestyle shots (show that vintage lamp in a stylish room setting)

Invest in a good camera or smartphone. Learn basic editing. Your bank account will thank you.

Customer Service: Your Brand in Action

You can have the coolest logo and the snazziest photos, but if your customer service sucks, so will your brand.

Some rules to live by:
- Respond quickly (like, really quickly)
- Be friendly but professional
- Go above and beyond (a handwritten thank-you note can turn a one-time buyer into a lifelong fan)

- Own your mistakes (we all make 'em, it's how you handle them that counts)

Remember: In the age of social media, one bad review can haunt you forever. Make every interaction count.

Social Media: Your 24/7 Brand Ambassador

Love it or hate it, social media is where it's at. But don't spread yourself too thin. Pick 1-2 platforms and rock them.

- Instagram: Perfect for visual sellers (fashion, home decor)
- TikTok: Great for behind-the-scenes and personality-driven brands
- Pinterest: Ideal for vintage and craft sellers

Don't just post your items. Share your process, your finds, your fails. People buy from people, not faceless entities.

Packaging: The Unboxing Experience

In a world of boring brown boxes, be a glitter bomb of joy.

Your packaging is the physical embodiment of your brand. Make it memorable.

Ideas:
- Custom tape or stickers with your logo
- Colorful tissue paper
- A branded thank-you card
- A small freebie (everyone loves a surprise)

Yes, it costs more. Yes, it's worth it. It's not just packaging; it's marketing.

Consistency: The Glue That Holds It All Together

This is where the rubber meets the road, folks. Your brand needs to be consistent across all touchpoints.

That means:
- Same logo everywhere
- Same color scheme
- Same tone of voice in all communications
- Same level of service, always

Consistency builds trust. Trust builds loyalty. Loyalty builds empires.

The Extra Mile: Surprise and Delight

Want to really make your brand stick? Go beyond expectations.

- Include a hand-picked bonus item with each order
- Remember your repeat customers' preferences
- Celebrate your customers' milestones (birthdays, anniversaries)

It's these little touches that turn customers into raving fans.

The Brand Audit: Keep Yourself Honest

Every few months, take a step back and look at your brand with fresh eyes.

- Is it still reflecting who you are and what you sell?
- Is it resonating with your target audience?
- Is it helping you stand out, or are you blending in?

Don't be afraid to evolve. The best brands grow with their business.

The Bottom Line

Building a brand isn't a one-and-done deal. It's an ongoing process, a living, breathing entity that grows with you.

It takes time. It takes effort. Sometimes, it takes money.

But here's the kicker: A strong brand is the difference between being a commodity and being irreplaceable. Between competing on price and commanding premium rates. Between being a seller and being a destination.

So roll up your sleeves, unleash your creativity, and let's build a brand that turns heads and opens wallets.

Chapter 6: The Power of Niche: Finding Your Reselling Sweet Spot

Let's talk about niches, baby.

In the wild world of reselling, being a jack-of-all-trades might seem smart. Cast a wide net, catch more fish, right? Wrong. Dead wrong.

Here's the truth: Specialization is where the real money's at.

Think about it. Would you rather be a small fish in a massive ocean or the big kahuna in a cozy lagoon? Yeah, thought so.

Niches are your ticket to the big leagues. They're how you go from "just another reseller" to "the go-to expert." But finding your niche? That's where things get tricky.

Why Niche Down?

1. Less competition. When you're selling everything under the sun, you're up against Amazon. Good luck with that.

2. Higher profits. Specialists can charge more. Period.

3. Repeat customers. Find your tribe, and they'll keep coming back for more.

4. Easier marketing. When you know exactly who you're selling to, reaching them becomes a piece of cake.

5. You become the expert. And experts make bank.

Finding Your Niche: It's Not Rocket Science (Unless That's Your Thing)

Here's the secret to finding your niche: Follow your passion... kind of.

Yes, passion matters. If you're not jazzed about what you're selling, you'll burn out faster than a cheap candle. But passion alone doesn't pay the bills.

You need the trifecta:
1. Something you love
2. Something you know (or can learn)
3. Something people will pay for

Let's break it down.

Love It or Leave It

What gets you excited? What can you talk about for hours without getting bored?

Maybe it's vintage cameras. Or mid-century furniture. Or obscure 90s toys.

Whatever it is, start there. Because when you love what you sell, it shows. And enthusiasm is contagious.

Knowledge is Power (and Profit)

You don't need to be a world-renowned expert from day one. But you should have a solid foundation.

Can you spot a fake from a mile away? Do you know which flaws are deal-breakers and which add character? Can you rattle off model numbers in your sleep?

If not, are you willing to learn? Because in niche reselling, knowledge isn't just power—it's cold, hard cash.

Show Me the Money

Here's where dreams meet reality. Is there actually a market for your niche?

Do some homework:
- Check eBay sold listings
- Scope out specialty forums
- Join Facebook groups dedicated to your niche

Look for items that sell consistently and for good prices. If you're seeing tumbleweeds, it might be time to pivot.

Niche Ideas to Get Your Gears Turning

- Vintage electronics (think: old iPods, game consoles, or hi-fi equipment)
- Rare books or first editions
- Vintage fashion from a specific decade
- Antique tools
- Movie props or memorabilia
- Discontinued makeup or perfume
- Vintage car parts
- Retro office supplies

The possibilities are endless. The key is to get specific. Really specific.

Testing the Waters: Dip Your Toes Before Diving In

Found a niche that ticks all the boxes? Great. Now, test it.

Start small. Source a few items. List them. See what happens.

Pay attention to:
- How quickly items sell
- Your profit margins
- Customer feedback
- How much you enjoy the process

If it's not working, don't be afraid to pivot. Better to change course early than to sink with a failing ship.

Expanding Your Niche: Growing Without Losing Focus

As you grow, you might be tempted to branch out. That's cool. But do it strategically.

Instead of jumping to a completely different niche, look for related areas. Selling vintage cameras? Maybe add in old photography books or antique photo albums.

The key is to expand in a way that makes sense to your existing customers. Give them more reasons to shop with you, not reasons to go elsewhere.

The Pitfalls of Niching Down (and How to Avoid Them)

Niching isn't all sunshine and rainbows. There are risks:

1. The market dries up. Trends change. Be ready to evolve.

2. You get bored. It happens. Keep things fresh by learning new aspects of your niche.

3. You pigeonhole yourself. Don't let your niche become a cage. It's okay to have side hustles.

4. You miss out on big scores outside your niche. Always keep your eyes open. A deal's a deal, niche or not.

The Secret Weapon of Niche Resellers: Community

Here's something the generalists miss out on: the power of community.

When you niche down, you're not just selling products. You're joining a tribe. Nurture it.

- Start a blog or YouTube channel about your niche
- Host meetups or virtual events
- Collaborate with other niche sellers (yes, even your "competition")

Building a community around your niche doesn't just drive sales. It creates a moat around your business that generalists can't touch.

The Bottom Line: Niche or Die

Okay, maybe that's a bit dramatic. But in a world where anyone can set up an online store in minutes, specialization is your secret weapon.

Find your niche. Own it. Become the expert. Build your tribe.

Do that, and you won't just survive in the reselling game. You'll thrive.

Chapter 7: Inventory Management: From Spare Room to Warehouse

Alright, reselling rockstars. You've been crushing it. Your spare room's bursting at the seams. Your partner's threatening divorce if they trip over one more box of vintage Beanie Babies. It's time to level up your inventory game.

Welcome to the wild world of inventory management. It's not sexy, but it's the backbone of your empire. Mess this up, and you're toast. Nail it, and you're on your way to the big leagues.

The Spare Room Squeeze

Let's start where most of us begin: the spare room (or closet, or garage, or under the bed – no judgment here).

When you're small, it's tempting to just chuck everything in a pile and call it a day. Don't. Future you will hate past you for this. Trust me.

Even in tight spaces, organization is key. Some quick wins:
- Clear plastic bins. Label 'em. Love 'em.
- Vacuum bags for clothes. Space-saving magic.
- Shelving units. Vertical space is your friend.
- A dedicated photo area. Even if it's just a corner.

Pro tip: Keep your best-selling items easily accessible. Nothing worse than digging through a mountain of stuff for that hot item that just sold.

The Great Spreadsheet Debate

Inventory tracking. Exciting, right? About as thrilling as watching paint dry. But skipping this step is like driving blindfolded. You might get lucky for a while, but eventually, you're gonna crash.

Options:
1. Good old Excel (or Google Sheets for the cloud lovers)
2. Dedicated inventory software
3. Your selling platform's built-in tools

Whatever you choose, track these basics:
- Item description
- Purchase date and cost
- Listed price
- Platform it's listed on
- Sold date and price (when it happens)

Feeling fancy? Add categories, conditions, and storage locations. Future you will buy past you a beer for this.

The Multi-Platform Juggling Act

Selling on eBay, Etsy, Poshmark, and your own website? Congrats, you're a circus performer now.

Cross-platform selling is great for maximizing exposure. It's also a recipe for overselling nightmares if you're not careful.

Some lifesavers:
- Use multi-platform management tools. They're worth every penny.
- Set up auto-updates across platforms when an item sells.

- Do regular inventory audits. Yes, it's a pain. Do it anyway.

Remember: A canceled sale due to out-of-stock items is worse than no sale at all. It's a reputation killer.

The Storage Unit Dilemma

Outgrown your home space? Welcome to the storage unit club. It's a rite of passage for growing resellers.

But beware: storage units can be money pits if you're not smart about it.

Tips for storage unit success:
- Choose climate-controlled units for delicate items.
- Organize like you're playing Tetris. Every inch counts.

- Visit regularly. Out of sight, out of mind = death to profits.
- Factor the cost into your item pricing. Seriously.

And for the love of all that's holy, don't forget to pay the bill. Storage unit auctions are fun to watch on TV. Less fun when it's your stuff on the block.

The Big League: Warehouse Space

Ready for the big time? Welcome to warehouse life.

This is where things get real. You're not just a reseller anymore. You're a logistics manager. Congrats?

Warehouse must-haves:

- A rock-solid inventory system. No more winging it.
- Proper shelving and storage solutions. Invest in good ones.
- A dedicated shipping area. Efficiency is king.
- Safety measures. Those piles of stuff can be treacherous.

Remember: With great space comes great responsibility (and overhead). Make sure your sales justify the upgrade.

The Inventory Audit: Your New Favorite Nightmare

Inventory audits. The reseller's equivalent of a root canal. Necessary, but oh so painful.

How often? Depends on your volume. Small operation? Quarterly might cut it. Big time? Monthly, or even weekly for fast-moving items.

Tips to make it less awful:

- Break it up into sections. Rome wasn't audited in a day.
- Use a barcode system. Your sanity will thank you.
- Get help. Pizza and beer can buy a lot of counting assistance.

Pro tip: Use this time to reassess your inventory. What's not moving? Time for a sale or a donation run.

The Art of Letting Go

Here's a hard truth: Not everything sells. Some stuff just sits there, taking up space and mocking your purchasing decisions.

Learn to let go. Set time limits. If it hasn't sold in 6 months (or whatever makes sense for your niche), it's time to cut bait.

Options for the non-movers:
- Slash prices. Sometimes, any profit is better than none.
- Bundle with popular items. Piggybacking works.
- Donate for a tax write-off. Your loss is someone's gain.
- Get creative. That ugly lamp might make a killer planter.

Remember: Holding onto dead stock is like carrying around a corpse. It's heavy, it stinks, and it's bad for business.

The Bottom Line: Systems Save Sanity

Inventory management isn't glamorous. It's not the fun part of reselling. But it's the difference between a hobby and a real business.

Invest time in setting up systems. Be ruthless about organization. Embrace the nerdy side of spreadsheets and barcodes.

Do this right, and you'll sleep better at night. You'll sell faster. You'll know exactly what you have and where it is.

And when that unicorn buyer asks if you have that rare widget in blue? You'll know in seconds. That's the power of good inventory management.

Chapter 8: Shipping and Handling: Streamlining Your Fulfillment Process

Alright, reselling warriors, it's time to tackle the beast that can make or break your business: shipping.

Ah, shipping. The necessary evil that can turn your profitable flip into a money pit faster than you can say "bubble wrap." But fear not! Master this dark art, and you'll be laughing all the way to the bank.

Let's dive in, shall we?

The Golden Rule of Shipping: Accuracy is King

Listen up, because this is crucial: Weigh. Your. Packages. Accurately.

Seriously. Don't eyeball it. Don't guess. And for the love of all that's holy, don't round down.

Invest in a good scale. Your options:
- Postal scale (for small items)
- Bathroom scale (for bigger stuff)
- Loading dock scale (for you big-time furniture flippers)

Underestimating weight is like playing Russian roulette with your profits. Sure, you might get away with it a few times. But when that postage due bill hits? Ouch.

Packaging Materials: Your New Best Friends

Welcome to the exciting world of bubble wrap and packing peanuts! Okay, it's not exciting. But it's necessary.

Pro tip: Start hoarding now. Your future self will thank you.

Essential supplies:
- Boxes (various sizes)
- Bubble wrap
- Packing paper
- Tape (lots of it)
- Poly mailers (for clothes and other soft items)

And here's a secret: You don't have to buy it all new. Reuse packaging from your personal purchases. Mother Earth and your wallet will both thank you.

The Great Debate: Free Shipping vs. Charged Shipping

Ah, the eternal question. To free ship, or not to free ship?

Here's the deal: Buyers love free shipping. They'll choose a $25 item with free shipping over a $20 item with $5 shipping every time. It's not logical, but it's reality.

But free shipping can eat into your profits faster than a moth in a cashmere store.

The solution? Build shipping into your prices. List that $20 item for $25 with "free" shipping. Everybody wins.

Just remember: If you're offering free shipping, calculate it into your costs. Don't let shipping fees be the silent killer of your business.

Carrier Wars: USPS vs. UPS vs. FedEx

Choosing a carrier is like picking a favorite child. They all have their strengths (and their annoying habits).

USPS:
- Great for small, lightweight items
- Flat rate boxes are your friend
- Generally cheapest for packages under 5 lbs

UPS:
- Better for larger, heavier items
- More reliable tracking
- Often cheaper for cross-country shipping

FedEx:
- Fast delivery times
- Good for urgent or valuable shipments
- Pricey, but sometimes worth it

Pro tip: Don't be loyal. Shop around. Use multiple carriers depending on the package. Your bottom line will thank you.

The Unboxing Experience: More Than Just Cardboard

Here's a mind-bender: Shipping isn't just about getting the item from A to B. It's part of your brand experience.

Think about it. The package arrival is often the first physical interaction a customer has with your brand. Make it count.

Some ideas:
- Custom packaging tape with your logo
- Thank you notes (handwritten for extra points)
- Small freebies (stickers, candy, etc.)

- Eco-friendly packaging for the environmentally conscious

Remember: In a world of boring brown boxes, be a glitter bomb of joy.

Insurance: Because Stuff Happens

Shipping insurance. It's like buying an umbrella. Seems unnecessary until it rains.

Here's the rule of thumb: If losing the item would hurt, insure it.

Yes, it cuts into your profits. But it beats having to refund a customer for a $500 item that mysteriously vanished in transit.

International Shipping: Here There Be Dragons

Thinking of going global? Brave soul. International shipping can be a goldmine... or a minefield.

Some tips for the intrepid:
- Research customs regulations. Every country's different.
- Use tracked shipping. Always.
- Be clear about who pays customs fees (hint: usually the buyer)
- Pad your handling time. International shipping can be slow.

Remember: The world is your oyster, but sometimes oysters give you food poisoning. Proceed with caution.

The Art of the Return

Returns. The bane of every reseller's existence. But they're a fact of life in this biz.

Your return policy can make or break your reputation. Be clear. Be fair. And for crying out loud, make it easy to find.

Some options:
- Free returns (builds trust, but can be costly)
- Buyer pays return shipping (saves you money, might deter some buyers)
- Store credit instead of refunds (keeps the money in your ecosystem)

Whatever you choose, stick to it. Consistency is key.

Automation: Your Secret Weapon

Here's a hard truth: You can't do it all yourself forever. As you grow, automation becomes your best friend.

Shipping software options:

- ShipStation
- Pirate Ship
- Shippo

These tools can:

- Import orders from multiple platforms
- Compare rates across carriers
- Print labels in bulk
- Send tracking info automatically

Yes, they cost money. But time is money, and these tools save you buckets of it.

The Bottom Line: Shipping Can Make or Break You

Here's the deal: You can source the best products, take the prettiest pictures, and write the most compelling listings. But if your shipping game is weak? It's all for naught.

Shipping is the last step in the transaction, but it's often the most remembered. A smooth shipping experience can turn a one-time buyer into a loyal customer. A bad one can sink your reputation faster than you can say "negative feedback."

So take it seriously. Invest time in streamlining your process. Stay organized. Be proactive in communicating with buyers about shipping.

Master this, and you'll be head and shoulders above the competition. Because in the end, it's not just about selling stuff. It's about delivering happiness, one package at a time.

Chapter 9: Customer Service: Turning Buyers into Repeat Customers

Let's get real for a second. You can have the coolest vintage finds, the slickest website, and shipping that'd make Amazon jealous. But if your customer service sucks? You're toast.

Welcome to the chapter that'll make or break your reselling empire: Customer Service.

The Golden Rule: Don't Be a Jerk

Sounds simple, right? You'd be surprised how many sellers forget this basic principle when a customer comes at them hot.

Here's the deal: People remember how you make them feel. And in the world of online selling, where face-to-face interaction is replaced by pixels on a screen, every word counts.

So, rule number one: Be nice. Even when the customer is wrong. Even when they're being unreasonable. Even when you want to reach through the screen and throttle them.

Why? Because kindness is your secret weapon. It disarms angry customers, encourages positive reviews, and turns one-time buyers into loyal fans.

Response Time: The Need for Speed

In the age of instant gratification, speed is king. Here's a hard truth: If you're not responding to customer inquiries within 24 hours (preferably much sooner), you're already behind.

Set up notifications. Check your messages obsessively. Heck, sleep with your phone if you have to (just kidding, don't do that. Work-life balance is a thing).

Pro tip: Can't reply in full right away? Send a quick "Got your message, working on it!" It buys you time and shows the customer you're on it.

The Art of the Apology

Screwed up? It happens. Maybe you shipped the wrong item. Maybe it arrived damaged. Maybe your dog ate the vintage baseball card (okay, that one's on you).

Here's how to apologize like a pro:

1. Own it. No excuses.
2. Say sorry. Actually use the word "sorry."
3. Make it right. Offer a solution.
4. Go above and beyond. A little extra effort here goes a long way.

Remember: A well-handled problem can actually create a more loyal customer than if nothing had gone wrong in the first place. Weird, but true.

The Power of Personalization

In a world of automated responses and chatbots, be human. Use the customer's name. Reference past purchases. Show them you see them as a person, not just a transaction.

Little touches go a long way:
- Handwritten thank-you notes
- Personalized product recommendations

- Remember their preferences for future interactions

It takes more time, sure. But it's what turns casual buyers into raving fans.

Handling the Karen (or Ken)

Ah, the dreaded difficult customer. Every seller's nightmare. But fear not! With the right approach, even the most Karen-est of Karens can be tamed.

The HEARD technique is your friend:
- Hear them out (let them vent)
- Empathize (show you understand their frustration)
- Apologize (even if it's not your fault)
- Resolve (offer a solution)
- Diagnose (figure out how to prevent it in the future)

Remember: Sometimes, people just want to be heard. A little empathy can go a long way.

The Feedback Game: Playing for Keeps

In the world of online selling, feedback is currency. Good reviews? They're gold. Bad ones? They're kryptonite.

So how do you stack the deck in your favor?

1. Ask for feedback. Many happy customers forget to leave reviews. A gentle reminder can work wonders.

2. Make it easy. Provide direct links to your feedback pages.

3. Respond to all feedback - good and bad. Thank the good. Address the bad (publicly and professionally).

4. Learn from criticism. Use negative feedback as free market research.

Pro tip: Got a bad review? Respond publicly with grace and offer to make it right. Future customers will see how well you handle problems.

The Extra Mile: Surprise and Delight

Want to create customers for life? Go beyond expectations.

Some ideas:
- Include a small freebie with each order
- Offer a discount on their next purchase

- Remember birthdays or purchase anniversaries

It's not about the monetary value. It's about showing you care. That you're not just another faceless online seller, but a real person who appreciates their business.

The Power of No (Nicely)

Here's a tough pill to swallow: You can't make everyone happy. Sometimes, you need to say no.

Maybe they want a refund outside your policy window. Maybe they're asking for a discount you can't afford to give. Whatever it is, learn to say no - firmly but kindly.

The key? Offer alternatives. Can't give a refund? Offer store credit. Can't match a competitor's price? Highlight your unique value proposition.

Remember: It's better to say no than to make promises you can't keep.

The Follow-Up: Don't Be a Stranger

The sale isn't over when you ship the item. Follow up. Make sure they're happy. Ask if they have any questions about their purchase.

It's not just good customer service. It's smart business. It opens the door for:
- Catching and fixing problems early
- Encouraging repeat purchases
- Getting valuable feedback

Plus, it shows you care beyond just making the sale. And that, my friends, is priceless.

The Bottom Line: Service is Your Superpower

In a world where anyone can set up an online store in minutes, customer service is your secret sauce. It's what sets you apart from the faceless masses of online sellers.

Great customer service isn't just about solving problems. It's about creating experiences. Building relationships. Turning transactions into connections.

Yes, it takes time. Yes, it takes effort. But the payoff? Loyal customers who not only come back again and again but sing your praises to others.

Remember: In the reselling game, your reputation is everything. Guard it fiercely.

Nurture it constantly. And watch your empire grow, one happy customer at a time.

Chapter 10: Scaling Up: From Side Hustle to Full-Time Business

Alright, reselling rockstar. You've been crushing it. Your spare room's bursting with inventory, your phone's blowing up with notifications, and you're starting to wonder: Can I really turn this side gig into my main squeeze?

Short answer: Hell yes.

Long answer: It's gonna take work. Blood, sweat, and maybe a few tears. But if you're ready to level up, buckle up. We're about to turn your hustle into a bonafide empire.

The Mindset Shift: Hobby to CEO

First things first: You gotta start thinking like a boss. Because guess what? You are one.

This isn't just about selling cool stuff anymore. It's about building a sustainable business. That means:

- Setting concrete goals (not just "make more money")
- Creating systems (because winging it doesn't scale)
- Making data-driven decisions (gut feelings are great, but numbers don't lie)

Time to put on your big kid pants and embrace your inner mogul.

The Numbers Game: Know Your Math or Go Home

Listen up, because this is crucial: You need to know your numbers. Cold.

We're talking:
- Profit margins (by item and overall)
- Operating costs (all of them, even the sneaky ones)
- Cash flow projections (because running out of cash is the kiss of death)

If math isn't your strong suit, time to make friends with spreadsheets. Or hire an accountant. Seriously. It'll be the best money you ever spent.

Time Management: Your New Superpower

Here's a hard truth: There are still only 24 hours in a day, even when you're the boss.

As you scale, time becomes your most precious resource. Guard it fiercely.

Some tips:
- Batch similar tasks (listing, shipping, sourcing)
- Use time-blocking techniques
- Learn to delegate (more on that in a sec)
- Automate everything you can

Remember: Working 80-hour weeks isn't sustainable. Work smarter, not just harder.

Delegation: You Can't Do It All (And You Shouldn't)

Letting go is hard. But if you want to scale, you gotta learn to delegate.

Start small:
- Hire a virtual assistant for customer service
- Get help with photography or listing

- Outsource your bookkeeping

Yes, it costs money. But it frees you up to focus on high-value tasks that actually grow your business.

Pro tip: Document your processes before you delegate. It'll make training way easier.

Diversify or Die: Expanding Your Reach

Putting all your eggs in one basket is risky business. As you scale, think about diversifying:

- Multiple selling platforms (don't rely solely on eBay or Etsy)
- Various product categories (in case one market tanks)
- Different sourcing methods (thrift stores, auctions, wholesale)

The goal? Create multiple income streams. It's like building a safety net for your business.

The Tech Stack: Tools of the Trade

As you grow, your toolkit needs to grow too. Invest in software that'll make your life easier:

- Inventory management systems
- Accounting software
- Social media scheduling tools
- Email marketing platforms

Yes, they cost money. But the time they save you? Priceless.

The Growth Mindset: Never Stop Learning

The market's always changing. Trends come and go. What worked yesterday might not work tomorrow.

To stay ahead, you gotta keep learning:
- Attend industry conferences
- Join online communities
- Read voraciously (blogs, books, industry reports)
- Consider getting a mentor

Remember: The day you stop learning is the day your business starts dying.

The Legal Stuff: Boring but Necessary

As you scale, you can't fly under the radar anymore. Time to get legit:

- Register your business
- Get proper insurance
- Understand tax obligations
- Consider trademarking your brand

Yeah, it's a snooze-fest. But it's crucial for protecting your growing empire.

The Work-Life Balance Tightrope

Here's the thing about turning your side hustle into a full-time gig: It's easy to let it consume your life.

Don't.

Set boundaries. Take days off. Remember why you started this in the first place.

A burnt-out boss is bad for business. Take care of yourself, and your business will thank you.

The Exit Strategy: Always Have a Plan

I know, I know. You're just scaling up. Why think about exiting?

Because smart business owners always have a plan. Whether it's:
- Selling the business
- Passing it on to family
- Or just having a "break glass in case of emergency" escape hatch

Knowing your end game helps you make better decisions along the way.

The Reality Check: It's Not All Sunshine and Rainbows

Scaling up is hard. There will be setbacks. Moments of doubt. Times when you wonder if you've made a huge mistake.

That's normal.

The difference between those who make it and those who don't? Persistence. Resilience. The ability to get back up when you get knocked down.

Remember: Every successful business owner has a story of almost quitting. Don't let that be the end of your story.

The Bottom Line: Dream Big, Start Small

Turning your side hustle into a full-time business isn't about making one big leap. It's about taking a series of small, calculated steps.

Start with a solid foundation. Build systems that can scale. Surround yourself with people who support your vision.

And most importantly? Believe in yourself. Because if you don't believe in your business, why should anyone else?

Chapter 11: Leveraging Social Media for Sales and Marketing

Welcome to the digital thunderdome, reselling warriors. It's time to talk social media.

Love it or hate it, social media is the heavyweight champion of modern marketing. Ignore it at your peril. Master it, and watch your reselling empire soar.

But here's the kicker: It's not just about posting pretty pictures and crossing your fingers. It's about strategy, consistency, and yes, a dash of shameless self-promotion.

Ready to turn those likes into cold, hard cash? Let's dive in.

Pick Your Poison: Choosing the Right Platforms

First things first: You can't be everywhere. Well, you can try, but you'll probably end up a burnt-out husk of a human. Not cute.

Instead, focus on the platforms where your ideal customers hang out. Selling vintage clothes? Instagram and Pinterest are your jam. Flipping electronics? YouTube and Twitter might be more your speed.

Do your homework. Spy on your competitors. See where the action is. Then plant your flag and own it.

The Content Conundrum: What the Heck Do I Post?

Here's a secret: People don't want to be sold to. They want to be entertained, educated, and inspired.

So mix it up:
- Behind-the-scenes peeks (everyone loves a good origin story)
- Tips and tricks related to your niche
- User-generated content (let your customers do the talking)
- The occasional shameless product plug (hey, you're running a business here)

Remember: You're not just selling products. You're selling a lifestyle, a vision, a slice of cool that your followers want to be part of.

The Art of the Hashtag: #DontScrewThisUp

Hashtags are like the secret sauce of social media. Use them right, and you'll tap into ready-made audiences. Use them wrong, and... crickets.

Some hashtag wisdom:
- Research trending tags in your niche
- Create a branded hashtag (and use it consistently)
- Don't go overboard (Instagram might love 30 hashtags, but on Twitter, that's just tacky)

Pro tip: Mix popular hashtags with niche-specific ones for maximum reach.

Consistency is Key: Showing Up When You Don't Feel Like It

Here's a hard truth: Social media success doesn't happen overnight. It's a long game, folks.

Set a posting schedule and stick to it. Whether it's daily, three times a week, or twice a day, consistency builds trust and keeps you top-of-mind.

But don't sacrifice quality for quantity. Better to post one killer piece of content a week than seven mediocre ones.

Engagement: It's Not a Monologue, It's a Conversation

Social media isn't a megaphone. It's a telephone. A two-way street. A... you get the idea.

Don't just broadcast. Engage. Respond to comments. Ask questions. Run polls. Slide into those DMs (professionally, of course).

The more you interact, the more the algorithms will love you. And the more your followers will see you as a real person, not just another faceless brand.

The Power of Video: Show, Don't Just Tell

If a picture's worth a thousand words, a video's worth a million. And in the attention economy, that's pure gold.

Try:
- Quick unboxing videos
- How-to tutorials related to your products
- Live Q&A sessions
- Behind-the-scenes glimpses of your sourcing adventures

Don't stress about production value. Authenticity trumps perfection every time.

Influencer Partnerships: Riding the Coattails of the Cool Kids

Influencers. Love 'em or hate 'em, they can skyrocket your reach overnight.

But here's the catch: You don't need the Kardashians. Micro-influencers (those with 1,000-100,000 followers) often have more engaged audiences and cheaper rates.

Look for influencers who align with your brand values. And always, always disclose sponsored content. The FTC doesn't mess around.

Paid Advertising: When Organic Just Isn't Cutting It

Organic reach is great, but sometimes you gotta pay to play. Social media ads can be a game-changer when done right.

Start small. Test different ad formats, copy, and targeting. Track your results obsessively. Scale what works, ditch what doesn't.

And for the love of all that's holy, don't blow your entire budget on one campaign. Slow and steady wins the race.

Analytics: Because Guessing is for Chumps

If you're not tracking your social media metrics, you're flying blind. And in the cutthroat world of reselling, that's a recipe for disaster.

Pay attention to:
- Engagement rates
- Click-through rates
- Conversion rates
- Follower growth

Most platforms offer built-in analytics. Use them. Love them. Let them guide your strategy.

The Art of the Soft Sell: Don't Be That Guy

Nobody likes a pushy salesperson, online or off. The key to social media success? Provide value first, sell second.

The 80/20 rule is a good starting point: 80% valuable, entertaining content, 20% sales pitches.

Remember: You're building relationships, not just making transactions.

Crisis Management: When Sht Hits the Fan

Sooner or later, you'll mess up. You'll ship the wrong item, post something insensitive, or get caught in a Twitter storm.

Have a plan ready:

1. Respond quickly
2. Be honest and transparent
3. Offer a genuine apology (if warranted)
4. Provide a solution
5. Learn from the experience

How you handle a crisis can make or break your brand. Stay cool, stay professional, and remember: This too shall pass.

The Bottom Line: Social Media is a Tool, Not a Magic Wand

Here's the deal: Social media can be a powerful ally in your reselling journey. But it's not a substitute for good products, fair prices, and stellar customer service.

Use it wisely. Use it consistently. But don't expect it to do all the heavy lifting.

Your reselling success still comes down to you: Your hustle, your vision, your ability to spot a deal and make a customer's day.

Social media is just the megaphone that lets the world know you've arrived.

Chapter 12: Financial Management: Tracking Profits and Planning for Growth

Alright, numbers nerds and math-phobes alike, it's time to talk cold, hard cash. Buckle up, because this might just be the chapter that makes or breaks your reselling empire.

Let's face it: You didn't get into this game to become an accountant. You're here for the thrill of the hunt, the satisfaction of a good flip, the sweet sound of ka-ching in your bank account. But here's the brutal truth: If you can't manage your money, you might as well pack up your inventory and call it quits now.

Don't panic. We're gonna break this down, piece by piece, until you're swimming in profit like Scrooge McDuck. (Minus the diving into a pool of coins. That stuff hurts.)

The Profit Equation: It's Not Rocket Science (But It's Close)

First things first: You gotta know your numbers. And I mean really know them. Not just a vague "I think I'm making money" feeling.

Here's the basic formula:
Profit = (Selling Price - Cost of Goods) - Expenses

Sounds simple, right? But let's break it down:

1. Selling Price: What the customer pays, including shipping.

2. Cost of Goods: What you paid for the item, plus any costs to get it ready for sale (cleaning, repairs, etc.).

3. Expenses: Everything else. Shipping costs, platform fees, packaging materials, that fancy coffee you need to fuel your late-night listing sessions.

Pro tip: Track every penny. Every. Single. One. That $2 bubble mailer might seem insignificant, but it adds up.

Cashflow: The Lifeblood of Your Business

Here's a fun fact: You can be profitable on paper and still go bankrupt. How? Poor cashflow management.

Cashflow is like oxygen for your business. Run out, and you're gasping for air, unable to buy inventory or pay your bills.

Some cashflow wisdom:

- Don't tie up all your capital in inventory. Keep a cushion.
- Plan for seasonal fluctuations. December might be booming, but what about the summer slump?
- Consider a business line of credit for those can't-miss bulk buying opportunities.

Remember: Cash is king. Treat it with the respect it deserves.

Bookkeeping: Embrace Your Inner Nerd

I get it. Bookkeeping is about as exciting as watching paint dry. But it's the foundation of your financial empire.

You've got options:

1. DIY with spreadsheets (cheap but time-consuming)
2. Use accounting software like QuickBooks or Wave (more efficient, slight learning curve)
3. Hire a bookkeeper (pricey, but frees up your time)

Whatever you choose, consistency is key. Set aside time each week to update your books. Future you will thank present you when tax season rolls around.

Taxes: The Necessary Evil

Speaking of taxes... let's rip off this Band-Aid.

As a reseller, you're likely considered self-employed. That means:
- Quarterly estimated tax payments
- Self-employment tax on top of income tax
- Keeping meticulous records for deductions

Don't mess with the IRS. They're not known for their sense of humor.

Consider working with a tax professional, at least for your first year. The peace of mind is worth every penny.

Pricing Strategy: The Art and Science of Making Bank

We talked about pricing in an earlier chapter, but it bears repeating: Your pricing strategy can make or break your profitability.

Some things to consider:
- Know your market. What are competitors charging?
- Factor in all your costs, including your time.
- Don't be afraid to price high for unique or in-demand items.

- Use psychological pricing tactics (e.g., $39.99 instead of $40)

Remember: You're not Walmart. You don't need to be the cheapest. You need to provide value.

Reinvestment: Fueling Your Growth

Here's where the rubber meets the road: How much of your profit should you plow back into the business?

There's no one-size-fits-all answer, but here's a guideline:
- 50% reinvestment
- 30% pay yourself
- 20% savings/taxes

Adjust as needed, but always, always pay yourself. You're building a business, not a really expensive hobby.

Financial Planning: Crystal Ball Not Required

You can't predict the future, but you can plan for it. Create financial projections for the next 6-12 months. Include:
- Expected revenue
- Anticipated expenses
- Cashflow forecasts

Will they be 100% accurate? Nope. But they'll give you a roadmap and help you spot potential issues before they become crises.

Key Performance Indicators (KPIs): Your Business Dashboard

KPIs are like the vital signs of your business. They tell you at a glance how healthy your operation is.

Some KPIs to track:
- Gross profit margin
- Inventory turnover rate
- Average order value
- Customer acquisition cost

Pick a few that matter most to your business and monitor them religiously.

The Emergency Fund: Your Business Lifesaver

Here's a scenario: Your top-selling product gets discontinued. Or a global pandemic shuts down your main sourcing spots. (Hey, it could happen...)

This is why you need an emergency fund. Aim for 3-6 months of operating expenses, tucked away in a high-yield savings account.

It's not sexy, but it might just save your business one day.

Scaling Smart: Don't Let Success Sink You

As you grow, your financial needs will change. Be prepared to:
- Upgrade your accounting systems
- Hire financial help (bookkeeper, accountant, CFO)
- Seek outside funding (loans, investors) if needed

Growing too fast can be just as dangerous as not growing at all. Keep a close eye on your numbers as you scale.

The Bottom Line: Money Matters

Look, I get it. You'd rather be out there hustling, finding the next big score. But neglect your finances, and all that hustle will be for nothing.

Treat your money with respect. Learn to love your numbers (or at least tolerate them). Because at the end of the day, this is a business, not a hobby.

Master your finances, and you'll have the freedom to build the reselling empire of your dreams. Ignore them, and... well, let's not go there.

Chapter 13: Navigating Legal and Tax Considerations for Resellers

Alright, reselling rockstars, it's time to put on your big kid pants. We're diving into the wild world of legal and tax considerations. I know, I know – about as exciting as watching paint dry, right? But trust me, this stuff is crucial. Ignore it at your peril.

Let's face it: The government wants its piece of the pie. And if you're not careful, that piece might be bigger than you bargained for. So buckle up, buttercup. We're about to navigate the treacherous waters of legalities and taxes.

The Business Structure Conundrum

First things first: What kind of business are you, legally speaking? Your options:

1. Sole Proprietorship: Easy peasy, but you're personally on the hook if things go south.
2. LLC (Limited Liability Company): More protection, a bit more paperwork.
3. Corporation: Big league stuff, probably overkill for most resellers.

Choose wisely, grasshopper. Your business structure affects everything from taxes to personal liability.

Pro tip: Chat with a lawyer or accountant before making this decision. It's worth the investment.

Licenses and Permits: The Necessary Evil

Depending on where you live and what you're selling, you might need some official paperwork. We're talking:

- Business licenses
- Sales tax permits
- Home occupation permits (if you're running this show from your living room)

Don't assume you're too small to need these. The government doesn't care if you're flipping Beanie Babies or Bentleys. Rules are rules.

Sales Tax: The Bane of Every Reseller's Existence

Ah, sales tax. The gift that keeps on giving (to the government, that is).

Here's the deal: If you're selling physical goods, you probably need to collect and remit sales tax. But it's not as simple as slapping on a flat percentage. Oh no, that would be too easy.

You need to consider:
- Where you have nexus (fancy word for a significant presence)
- Different rates for different states, counties, even cities
- Which items are taxable (it varies by location)

Feeling overwhelmed yet? Yeah, welcome to the club.

Income Tax: Uncle Sam Wants His Cut

Remember when you got a regular paycheck and taxes were automatically deducted? Those were the days, huh?

As a reseller, you're likely considered self-employed. That means:

- You're responsible for paying your own income tax
- You need to make quarterly estimated tax payments
- You'll pay self-employment tax on top of income tax

Fun times, right? But wait, there's more!

Deductions: Your Secret Weapon

Here's where things get interesting. As a business owner, you can deduct a whole bunch of expenses. We're talking:

- Cost of goods sold
- Home office expenses
- Mileage for sourcing trips
- Shipping supplies
- Even that fancy camera you use for product photos

But here's the catch: You need to keep meticulous records. Every receipt, every mile driven, every penny spent. The IRS isn't big on the honor system.

Recordkeeping: Your New Favorite Hobby

Speaking of records, get ready to channel your inner librarian. You'll need to keep:

- Sales records
- Expense receipts
- Inventory logs
- Bank statements
- Tax returns (for at least 3 years)

Invest in a good filing system. Your sanity (and your accountant) will thank you.

The Online Marketplace Maze

Selling on eBay, Amazon, or Etsy? They've got their own set of rules and regulations. Some fun facts:

- eBay will send you a 1099-K if you sell over $20,000 or have 200+ transactions
- Amazon collects sales tax in many states on your behalf (but not all!)
- Etsy requires you to have a separate bank account for your shop

Read those terms of service, folks. Ignorance isn't bliss when it comes to marketplace policies.

Intellectual Property: Don't Be a Copycat

Just because you can find a knockoff Louis Vuitton doesn't mean you should sell it. Trademark and copyright laws are no joke.

Be particularly careful with:
- Designer brands
- Licensed character merchandise
- Anything with a logo you didn't create

When in doubt, stick to authentic goods. Your legal budget will thank you.

Consumer Protection Laws: Because Customers Have Rights Too

As a seller, you've got responsibilities to your buyers. We're talking:

- Accurate product descriptions
- Fair pricing practices
- Reasonable return policies
- Protecting customer data

Violate these, and you're not just risking bad reviews. You could be facing legal action.

The International Twist

Thinking of selling globally? Buckle up for a whole new level of complexity.

You'll need to navigate:
- Customs regulations
- International shipping laws
- VAT (Value Added Tax) in many countries
- Currency exchange considerations

It's not for the faint of heart, but the global market can be lucrative if you do it right.

When to Call in the Pros

Look, I get it. You got into this business to make money, not spend it on lawyers and accountants. But sometimes, professional help is worth its weight in gold.

Consider getting expert advice for:
- Setting up your business structure
- Navigating complex tax situations
- Dealing with legal disputes
- Annual tax preparation

Think of it as an investment in your business's future.

The Bottom Line: CYA (Cover Your Assets)

Here's the deal: The legal and tax landscape for resellers is complex and ever-changing. What works today might not fly tomorrow.

Stay informed. Join reseller groups, follow relevant blogs, maybe even make friends with a tax pro.

And when in doubt, ask for help. It's better to spend a little money on good advice than a lot of money on fines and penalties.

Remember: You're not just a reseller. You're a business owner. Act like one.

Chapter 14: Advanced Flipping: Restoring and Upcycling for Higher Profits

Welcome to the big leagues, reselling maverick. If you've made it this far, you're no longer content with simply buying low and selling high. Oh no, you're ready to add some serious value to your finds and watch those profit margins soar. It's time to talk restoration and upcycling.

Buckle up, buttercup. We're about to turn trash into treasure, and make a killing doing it.

The Art of Seeing Potential

First things first: You need to develop your "potential vision." That ratty old dresser? It's not junk. It's a mid-century modern masterpiece waiting to happen. Those stained vintage clothes? Future statement pieces.

Train your eye to see past the dust, the rust, and the years of neglect. Look for good bones, quality materials, and timeless design. It's not about what an item is – it's about what it could be.

Tools of the Trade: Invest in Your Arsenal

You can't fight a war with a butter knife, and you can't restore antiques with a hammer and some duct tape. Time to build your toolkit:

- For furniture: Sanders, paint sprayers, wood filler, quality brushes
- For clothing: Sewing machine, fabric dyes, stain removers

- For electronics: Soldering iron, multimeter, specialized screwdrivers

Yes, it's an investment. But these tools will pay for themselves many times over.

Research: Know Your Stuff or Get Stuffed

Before you start slapping paint on that vintage radio, do your homework. What's period-appropriate? What techniques were used originally? What materials are safe to use?

Join restoration forums. Watch YouTube tutorials. Maybe even take a class or two. The more you know, the more valuable your restorations become.

The Fine Line: Restoration vs. Destruction

Here's a hard truth: Sometimes, less is more. Not every item needs a complete overhaul. In fact, over-restoring can actually decrease value, especially for antiques and collectibles.

Learn to discern:
- When to do a full restoration
- When a simple cleaning will suffice
- When to leave that patina alone

Remember: You're not erasing history. You're preserving it for the next generation.

Upcycling: Trash to Cash

Now, let's talk upcycling. This is where your creativity really gets to shine. Upcycling is about reimagining an item's purpose and giving it new life.

Some ideas to get your gears turning:

- Turn old doors into headboards
- Transform vintage suitcases into quirky side tables
- Use broken china to create mosaic art

The sky's the limit. The weirder, the better. People pay big bucks for unique, conversation-starting pieces.

Photography: Before and After Magic

In the world of restoration and upcycling, the transformation is everything. Your photography needs to tell that story.

Invest in good lighting. Take clear, well-composed "before" shots. Then knock their socks off with stunning "after" photos. Show your piece in context – stage it in a stylish room setting.

Remember: You're not just selling an item. You're selling a vision of what their space could look like.

Pricing: The Art of Knowing Your Worth

Here's where many restorers stumble. How do you price your blood, sweat, and tears?

Consider:
- Cost of materials
- Time invested (your labor has value!)
- Rarity of the original piece
- Quality of your restoration/upcycling work

Don't be afraid to price high. You're offering something unique. The right buyer will pay for quality and creativity.

Marketing: Tell Your Story

In the world of restored and upcycled goods, the story is half the sale. Where did you find the piece? What inspired your vision for it? What challenges did you overcome in the restoration process?

Use your item descriptions to paint a picture. Share progress photos on social media. Maybe even start a blog or YouTube channel documenting your projects.

People aren't just buying furniture or clothes. They're buying a piece of your artistic journey.

Specialization: Find Your Niche

As you dive deeper into the world of restoration and upcycling, consider specializing. Maybe you become the go-to person for:

- Art Deco lamp restorations

- Upcycled industrial furniture
- Vintage wedding dress renovations

Specialization allows you to hone your skills, build a reputation, and command higher prices.

Sustainability: The Green Angle

Here's a selling point you shouldn't overlook: Restoration and upcycling are eco-friendly practices. You're keeping items out of landfills and reducing the demand for new production.

Play up this angle in your marketing. Many buyers are willing to pay a premium for sustainable, ethically-sourced goods.

Collaborations: Two Heads are Better Than One

Don't be afraid to team up with other artists or craftspeople. Maybe you're great at finding and restoring pieces, but your painting skills are so-so. Partner with a local artist to create truly one-of-a-kind items.

Collaborations can lead to fresh ideas, expanded skillsets, and new customer bases.

Legal Considerations: Cover Your Bases

A quick word of caution: When you're significantly altering items, especially antiques, you need to be clear about what you've done. Misrepresenting a heavily restored piece as "original" can land you in hot water.

Be transparent about your restoration processes. It's not just ethical – it's often legally required.

The Bottom Line: Passion Pays

Here's the truth: Restoration and upcycling aren't get-rich-quick schemes. They require skill, patience, and a healthy dose of artistic vision. But for those willing to put in the work, the rewards can be substantial.

You're not just flipping items anymore. You're creating art. You're preserving history. You're turning neglected objects into cherished possessions.

And yes, you're making a tidy profit while doing it.

Chapter 15: Building a Team: When and How to Hire Help

Alright, hotshot. Your reselling empire is booming. You're drowning in inventory, your phone's blowing up with customer inquiries, and you haven't seen your family in what feels like years. Congrats! You've hit the sweet spot where success meets overwhelm.

It's time to face facts: You can't do it all alone anymore. Welcome to the wild world of building a team.

The Solo-preneur's Dilemma

First, let's address the elephant in the room. Hiring help is scary. It means letting go of control, trusting others with your baby, and -

gulp – actually being responsible for someone else's paycheck.

But here's the truth bomb: If you want to grow, you gotta let go. Your business can only scale as far as your two hands can take it. After that, it's team time, baby.

Signs You're Ready to Hire

Not sure if you're there yet? Look for these red flags:
1. You're turning down opportunities because you're too swamped.
2. Quality is slipping because you're stretched too thin.
3. You're working 80-hour weeks and still falling behind.
4. Simple tasks are falling through the cracks.

5. You're missing out on family time, sleep, or basic hygiene. (Seriously, when was the last time you showered?)

If you're nodding along, congratulations! You're ready to join the ranks of job creators.

What to Hire For: Identifying Your Weak Spots

Before you start plastering "Help Wanted" signs all over town, take a step back. What tasks are eating up your time? What are you honestly not great at?

Common first hires for resellers:
- A photographer (because your iPhone shots just aren't cutting it anymore)
- A shipper/inventory manager (farewell, late-night packing sessions)

- A customer service rep (to handle those "where's my order?" emails)
- A bookkeeper (because numbers make your head spin)

Pro tip: Start with your biggest pain point. What task do you dread most? That's probably where you need help first.

The Great Debate: Employee vs. Contractor

Now for some thrilling legal stuff! (Just kidding, it's about as exciting as watching paint dry. But it's important, so pay attention.)

You've got two main options:
1. Employees: More control, more legal obligations, more expensive.
2. Independent Contractors: More flexibility, fewer legal hoops, but less control.

Each has its pros and cons. Employees are great for long-term, consistent work. Contractors are perfect for project-based or fluctuating workloads.

When in doubt, consult a lawyer or HR pro. The IRS doesn't mess around with misclassification.

Where to Find Your Dream Team

Great, you know what you need. Now where do you find these magical helpers?

- Online job boards (Indeed, LinkedIn, etc.)
- Freelance platforms (Upwork, Fiverr)
- Local colleges (hello, eager interns!)
- Your own customer base (they already know your business!)

Cast a wide net, but be specific in your job descriptions. You want quality candidates, not a flood of unqualified resumes.

The Art of the Interview: Don't Screw This Up

Interviewing is like dating. You're looking for the right fit, someone you can stand being around for hours on end.

Some tips:
- Be clear about expectations (hours, pay, duties)
- Ask scenario-based questions ("How would you handle a customer who...")
- Look for culture fit (can they vibe with your quirky reselling world?)
- Trust your gut (if something feels off, it probably is)

Remember: You're not just hiring skills. You're hiring a person. Make sure they're someone you actually want to work with.

Training: Don't Throw 'Em to the Wolves

Congrats! You've hired your first team member. Now the real work begins.

Resist the urge to dump everything on them and run. Proper training is crucial. Document your processes, create training materials, and be patient. Yes, it's time-consuming. No, you can't skip this step.

Remember: Every minute you invest in training now saves you hours of headaches later.

Delegation: The Art of Letting Go

Here's where many first-time bosses stumble. You've got help, but you're still doing everything yourself. What gives?

Delegation is a skill. It takes practice. Start small. Give clear instructions. Provide feedback. And for the love of all that's holy, resist the urge to micromanage.

Your mantra: If you want it done right, teach someone else to do it right.

Creating a Positive Work Culture (Even if "Work" is Your Garage)

News flash: Happy workers are productive workers. Even if your "office" is your spare bedroom, you can create a positive work environment.

Some ideas:

- Regular check-ins (show you care about their input)
- Clear communication (no one likes guessing games)
- Recognition for good work (a little praise goes a long way)
- Opportunities for growth (help them level up their skills)

Remember: Your team is investing their time in your dream. Make it worth their while.

The Legal Stuff: Don't Skip This Part

Hiring comes with legal obligations. Exciting, right? (No, not really, but it's crucial.)

You'll need to think about:
- Payroll taxes
- Workers' comp insurance

- Employment laws (minimum wage, overtime, etc.)
- Safety regulations (even if you're working from home)

When in doubt, consult a pro. The money you spend on legal advice is way less than what you'd spend on fines or lawsuits.

Scaling Your Team: Growing Pains Are Real

As your business grows, so will your team. Be prepared for:
- Shifting roles (that jack-of-all-trades might become a specialist)
- New management layers (hello, middle management!)
- Evolving company culture (it changes as you grow)
- Increased complexity (more people = more moving parts)

Stay flexible. What works for a team of 2 might not work for a team of 20.

The Bottom Line: Your Team is Your Secret Weapon

Building a team isn't just about offloading tasks. It's about creating a force multiplier for your business.

A good team can take your vision and run with it, propelling your reselling empire to heights you never imagined.

Yes, it's scary. Yes, it's a lot of work. But done right, building a team is the key to unlocking the next level of your reselling success.

So take a deep breath, put on your boss pants, and get ready to lead. Your empire awaits, and it's too big for just one person to rule.

Copyright 2023
Silas Meadowlark

www.ingramcontent.com/pod-product-compliance
Lightning Source LLC
Chambersburg PA
CBHW031927240526
45464CB00023B/1905